THE FACTS ON ISLAM

John Ankerberg & John Weldon

HARVEST HOUSE PUBLISHERS
Eugene, Oregon 97402

Other books by
John Ankerberg and John Weldon

The Facts on Angels
The Facts on Astrology
The Facts on Creation vs. Evolution
The Facts on the Faith Movement
The Facts on False Teaching in the Church
The Facts on Halloween
The Facts on Holistic Health and the New Medicine
The Facts on Homosexuality
The Facts on the Jehovah's Witnesses
The Facts on the King James Only Debate
The Facts on the Masonic Lodge
The Facts on the Mormon Church
The Facts on the New Age Movement
The Facts on the Occult
The Facts on Roman Catholicism

THE FACTS ON ISLAM
Copyright © 1991 by "The John Ankerberg Show"
Revised 1998
Published by Harvest House Publishers
Eugene, Oregon 97402

ISBN 0-89081-913-0

Printed in the United States of America.

01 02 03 04 05 06 07 08 / VP / 17 16 15 14 13 12

CONTENTS

Preface

Section V
The Accuracy of the New Testament Text

Preface

Apart from Christianity, Islam is arguably the most influential religion on earth. It is the second largest religion in the world, and the powerful resurgence of Islamic fundamentalism continues to spread the Muslim faith in more moderate Islamic nations.

What is the difference between the terms "Islam" and "Muslim"?

"Islam" is the correct name for the religion that the Muslim prophet Muhammad claimed God (Allah) revealed to him through the angel Gabriel. The name is derived from the infinitive of the Arabic verb "to submit" (i.e., to Allah's will). "Muslim" is the correct term for a follower of Islam and comes from the present participle of the same verb.[1]

More than any other single factor, the followers of Islam have their lives directed by the book they believe is the Word of God—the Koran. Dr. J. Christy Wilson of Princeton University comments, "Next to the Bible, it is the most esteemed and most powerful book in the world."[2] Whatever Muslims believe and do, it is the teachings in the Koran that have inspired these beliefs and actions. This is why no one should underestimate the importance of the Koran.

The purpose of this booklet is first to supply a critique of Islam from the perspective of history and Christian faith, and second, to encourage persons familiar with this information to seek appropriate and effective ways of relating that information to their Muslim friends. The material in this booklet is introductory—primarily to inform Christians and non-Muslims about Islam as it relates both to Christian and Muslim truth claims.

Regrettably, Muslims often have a number of unfortunate misunderstandings concerning Christianity. Muslims may also be very sensitive to even valid criticisms about Islam, the Koran, or Muhammad, so dialogue can be difficult. Help on effectively relating to Muslims ("Dos" and "Don'ts," etc.) can be found in the note preceding our endnotes. We emphasize that any Christian desiring to minister to Muslims will find it helpful to continue studies in this direction.

Muslims may refuse to approve translations of the Koran. Nevertheless, a good English translation does provide sufficiently accurate meanings of the original. The translations we have chosen to cite are those by A.J. Arberry, which in the words of Wilfred Cantwell Smith of Harvard University, is "the one that comes closest to conveying the impression made on the Muslims by the original";[3] that of the Iranian scholar N.J. Dawood, director of *Contemporary Translation Limited* and managing director of the Arabic Advertising and Publishing Company, Ltd., London; that of J.M. Rodwell, which "has been declared by modern scholars to be one of the best translations ever produced";[4] and that by Abdullah Yusuf Ali, *The Holy Qur'an,* widely used among American Muslims and considered by them among the best of translations. Indeed, "some Muslims are prepared to commend the accuracy of the best of these translations, and to admit their value as interpretation, though not official interpretation, of the meaning of the sacred text."[5]

While Muslims may be critical of non-Muslim translations (as, e.g., Ali is of Rodwell's), one should not necessarily conclude Muslim translations are always more accurate. For example, "Muslim translators such as Yusuf Ali will not hesitate to mistranslate the Arabic text [cf. Sura 5:76] in order to keep the English reader from discovering obvious errors in the Quran....The readers of his translation must be aware of its hidden apologetic agenda."[6]

Finally, it should be noted that there are different traditions of Islam (e.g., Sunni, Shi'ite, and Sufi) and, correspondingly, quite different interpretations of the Koran.

Section I
The Religion of Islam: Introduction

1. What is Islam?

Islam is the world religion founded by an Arabian visionary named Muhammad (ca. 570–632 A.D.; var. sp.: Muhammed, Mohammed), who was born in the city of Mecca in Arabia. Muhammad claimed he received supernatural revelations from God through the angel Gabriel. These revelations were written down by others and compiled into a book called the Koran, the Muslim Bible (var. sp.: Quran).

Islam today is comprised of two principal schools—the majority Sunni school (90%) and the minority Shi'ite school (10%). In addition, there are millions of Muslim mystics called Sufis. In America, Muslim influence is seen in traditional Islam as well as the militant, racist black Muslim movement.[7] There are now between 5 and 8 million Muslims in America, and their numbers will apparently continue to expand for the foreseeable future.

2. Why is Islam important?

In brief, Islam is important for the following reasons. First, there are one billion followers of Islam in the world. Second, the collective power of Islam is able to dramatically influence the world economy through OPEC. Third, the growing religious influence of Islam outside Islamic nations is unmistakable. Fourth, Islam has the ability to play a key role in the social stability or instability of dozens of governments around the world. Fifth, a principal goal of Islam is to bring Islamic law to every nation.[8]

Islam is important because it has the power to change the destinies of hundreds of millions of people— and perhaps the West itself. Further, Arab nationalism and the Muslim religion have become the single most crucial issue in the volatile Middle East, now a focal point for the attention of the entire world. No one can know how a major crisis in that region may ultimately affect the rest of the world. But the possibilities are sobering.[9]

The influence of Islam in the modern world is increasing daily in other ways. With its recent rise to more than one billion people in membership, it claims to be the fastest growing religion in the world, and it dominates more than 40 countries on three continents. It is the driving force behind numerous nations in the Middle East, Africa, and Asia. Indeed, well over 30 countries now have populations that are at least 87% Muslim. It has also become the second largest religion in Europe and the third largest in the U.S. Islam is now Britain's third largest religion. In 1974, France had one mosque—today there are more than 1,600. There are now more Muslims than Methodists in Chicago and more than 500,000 in Los Angeles alone. All told, in the U.S. there are more than 1,000 mosques and Islamic centers, some 400 Muslim student organizations, and dozens of professional organizations.[10]

Finally, the ideological influence of Islam expands to other nations on a daily basis, and Islamic fundamentalism is increasingly aggressive. Religiously, socially, politically, economically, and militarily, Islam will continue to powerfully impact our world. For example, Christian readers of this booklet should not think Islam is of little concern to the Church. The January 1996 World Watch Persecution Index, published by Open Doors, revealed that, apart from North Korea and China, Islamic-dominated countries occupied every single spot on the top ten list of countries where persecution of Christians is most severe. Some of the reasons for this unfortunate situation will become evident as we proceed.

3. How did Islam begin?

Islam began with the supernatural visions and revelations that Muhammad claimed he received from God through the angel Gabriel beginning in 610 A.D. Because Muhammad was uneducated and could neither read nor write, these revelations were first memorized and then later written down by his followers. The authoritative *Cambridge History of Islam* discusses these revelations by noting that "either in the course of the visions or shortly afterwards, Muhammad began to receive 'messages' or 'revelations' from God....He believed that he could easily distinguish between his own thinking and these revelations.... Muhammad continued to receive the messages at intervals until his death." [11]

In addition to the revelations, the personality of Muhammad played an important role in the success of Islam. His character was both complex and contradictory. Sir Norman Anderson studied law at Cambridge, and Arabic and Islamic law at the University of Cairo. He is considered an authority on both comparative religion and Islamic law and teaches at the University of London. In *The World's Religions*, he describes the temperament of Muhammad: "The adult Muhammad soon showed signs of a markedly religious disposition. He would retire to caves for seclusion and meditation; he frequently practiced fasting; and he was prone to [revelationary] dreams....He was generous, resolute, genial, and astute: a shrewd judge and a born leader of men. He could, however, be cruel and vindictive to his enemies: he could stoop to assassination; and he was undeniably sensual.[12] One of the leading biographers of our modern era, Robert Payne, observes that "violence and gentleness were at war within him."[13]

In conclusion, Islam began as a consequence of supernatural revelations received by Muhammad. Whatever Islam has accomplished historically, whatever it is today, it results largely from these supernatural revelations received by Muhammad some 1,400 years ago.

However, at the end of his life, Muhammad failed to name a successor. This failure resulted in the major division of Islam into the majority Sunni and minority Shi'ite branches, each claiming to be true Islam. These divisions disagree as to the legitimate successor of Muhammad and over who offers the most accurate representation of Islamic faith.[14]

4. What are the basic Muslim beliefs?

Every Muslim must hold to six basic beliefs or articles of Islamic faith. They are:

Faith in Allah

Muslims believe there is only one true God and that his name is Allah. His will is supreme.

Angels

Muslims believe in angels—such as "Gabriel," who allegedly transmitted the Koran to Muhammad.

The Holy Books

Muslims believe that Allah has given a long series of revelations, including the Old and New Testaments. But these revelations end with the Koran, which supersedes and to a large degree abrogates the others. For all practical purposes, Muslims accept only the Koran as the Word of God. For example, they believe Allah's earlier revelations in the Bible have been corrupted and/or falsely interpreted by Jesus and Christians, so the Koran is needed for proper understanding.

(Because Muslims rely on this idea so heavily in their interaction with Christians, we have provided documentation showing why the New Testament documents are accurate and truthful. If they choose to deal fairly with the historical evidence, Muslims must logically accept the reliability of the New Testament text [see Q. 18].)

The Prophets

Muslims believe Allah has sent 124,000 prophets to mankind, although only about 25 are mentioned in the Koran. Six of the principal prophets are Adam, the chosen of Allah; Noah, the preacher of Allah; Abraham, the friend of Allah; Moses, the speaker of Allah; Jesus, the word of Allah; and Muhammad, the apostle of Allah.

Because Muhammad's revelation is considered the greatest of all, he is called the "Seal of the Prophets," "Peace of the World," and given more than 200 other appellations.

Predestination

Muslims believe everything that happens, both good and evil, is predestined by Allah's will, his immutable decree.

The Day of Judgment

Muslims believe that on this day the good and evil deeds of men will be placed on a "scale." Those Muslims having sufficient personal merit and righteousness (and the favor of Allah) will go to eternal heaven; all others will go to eternal hell.

These required articles of faith are also related to specific Muslim practices.

5. *What religious duties are required of all Muslims?*

Every Muslim must practice at least five fundamental religious duties. These are known as the "Pillars of Religion." They are considered obligatory observances upon which the Muslim faith rests.

The first is reciting the creed of Islam—"There is no God but Allah and Muhammad is his prophet."

The second involves prayer. The Muslim must recite prescribed prayers five times a day. Each time he must adopt a physical posture: standing, kneeling, hands and face to the ground, etc. The call to prayer is sounded by a Muslim *muezzin* (crier) from a tower called a *minaret*. This is part of the Muslim church or public place of worship called the *mosque*.

The third religious duty is observing the month of fasting called *Ramadan*. This fast commemorates the first revelation of the Koran that Mohammad received in

610 A.D. Although eating is permitted at night, for an entire month Muslims must fast during the day.

The fourth pillar of Islamic duty is the giving of alms to the poor. Muslims are required to give 2.5% of their currency plus other forms of wealth, as determined by a complicated system.

The fifth and last duty is that of a pilgrimage to Mecca, Muhammad's place of birth. This is required at least once during the lifetime of every Muslim who is physically and financially able to make the trip (unless he is a slave).

A sixth religious duty is often associated with the above five pillars, although it is considered optional by some. This is the Muslim holy war or *jihad*. Jihad may be interpreted as internal (as spiritual struggle) or external (defending Islam). When the situation warrants it, this duty requires Muslims to go to war to defend Islam against its enemies. Anyone who dies in a holy war is allegedly guaranteed eternal life in heaven and is considered a martyr for Islam.

For example, Saddam Hussein attempted to gather support for his takeover of Kuwait and his war against America by issuing a call to Muslims for a holy war against the West. Although this largely failed because of Hussein's blatant secularism, it did not fail entirely. The end result was over 100 terrorist actions committed against America and Western interests in the first month of the war, not to mention massive demonstrations against the West in many Islamic countries.

Section II
The Theology of Islam: Is It Compatible with Christian Belief?

6. *What does Islam teach about Allah, and is he like the God of the Bible?*

Islam teaches that the true God is the Muslim deity, Allah. All other views of God are false because the Koran teaches, "The true religion with God is Islam."[15] The Koran emphasizes of Allah: "There is no God but he, the Living, the everlasting."[16]

But who is Allah? Is he anything like the God of Christian faith? As we will see, the Muslim God is entirely different from the biblical God. First, the Koran stresses that Allah is one person only: "They are unbelievers who say, 'God is the Third of Three.' No god is there but one God. If they refrain not from what they say, there shall afflict those of them that disbelieve a painful chastisement."[17] Here, the Koran emphasizes that Christians are unbelievers because they accept the historic Christian doctrine of the Trinity.[18] But, as we fully documented in our *Knowing the Truth About the Trinity* (Harvest House, 1997), the Bible unmistakably tells us that God has revealed Himself as a triune Being, as One God eternally existing in three Persons—Father, Son, and Holy Spirit (Mt. 28:19; Jn. 1:1,14; Acts 5:3-4).[19] Although many Muslims believe otherwise, Christians do *not* believe in three gods. This idea is a clear misrepresentation of Christian belief. Christians are not polytheists, who accept three gods, but monotheists who believe in one God.

Second, the Muslim God has a different character than the biblical God. It is significant that of the "99 beautiful names for Allah," which Muslims memorize and use for worship, not one of these names is "love" or "loving." The Koran stresses that Allah only "loves" those who do good, but that he does not love those who are bad. Allah himself emphasizes that he does *not* love the sinner.[20] Thus, the love of Allah is not the love of the God of the Bible. The biblical God does love the sinner— in fact, He loves all sinners. God does not love the sin, but He does love the sinner: "Christ died for the *ungodly*....God *demonstrates* his own *love* for us in this: while we were *still sinners,* Christ died for us....If when we were God's *enemies,* we were reconciled to him through the death of his Son, how much more, having been reconciled, shall we be saved through his life?" (Rom. 5:6,8,10). Essentially, Allah is primarily a God of power, not a God of love. But the Bible declares, "God *is* love" (1 Jn. 4:6).

Next, through predestination of all things, Allah is considered the direct author of *both* good and evil. This is not the God of the Bible. While the biblical God is sovereign and permits evil, He is not its direct cause. Even when it is part of His plan, He frequently turns it to a higher good, as seen in the death of Jesus for our sins, Joseph being sold into slavery (Gen. 45:8; 50:20), and in Romans 8:28: "And we know that in all things God works for the good of those who love him, who have been called according to his purpose." Again, the biblical God is not the direct author of evil. Rather, He is infinitely holy and righteous (1 Sam. 2:2; Ps. 77:13; 99:9; Rev. 15:4), and His "eyes are too pure to look on evil" (Hab. 1:3).

Third, Allah is ultimately unknowable and incomprehensible. In *Who Is Allah in Islam,* Abd-al-Masih writes, "Allah is the unique, unexplorable, and inexplicable one—the remote, vast, and unknown God. Everything we think about him is incomplete, if not wrong. Allah cannot be comprehended."[21]

In "What Is Allah Like?" George Houssney writes, "We humans can never know Allah, because he is so far from us and so different from us. The only knowledge Muslims may admit to is knowledge about Allah, not a personal, experiential knowledge of him. People cannot know Allah and should not even try to know him. Allah is not involved in the affairs of humans." Thus, Houssney goes on to point out the contrast between Muslim and Christian concepts concerning humanity's relationship to God: "The Christian claim that humans can have a relationship with God is considered by Muslims to be a metaphysical impossibility. To Muslims, Allah has not revealed himself, but rather he has revealed his *mashi'at* (desires and wishes, i.e., his will). His will, according to Islamic teaching, is limited to Islamic law. A person performs the will of Allah when he follows the dictates of the Islamic legal system."* Finally, Houssney further illustrates the distinction between Muslim and Christian concepts of God at this point: "Allah has no personality and is indescribable by any characteristic attributable to man. Most of his attributes are absolute qualities which are unique to himself, like adjectives of majesty. Although some of his attributes may appear to be relational, such as mercy, they are nonmutual and one-directional. According to the Islamic doctrine of Allah, he is nonrelational. To claim that Allah is relational is to make him dependent on his creation."[22]

All this stands in contrast to the biblical teaching that men and women *can* know God personally on an intimate, relational level. Consider these Scriptures:

---

* This involves the Koran as *interpreted* by Muslim clerics; cf. Q. 17; to submit to the "will of Allah," is to submit to the religious leaders' interpretations of the Koran, which involve everything relating to life, including Islamic law, politics, cultural customs, family, etc. To submit to Allah is to submit to the Islamic powers that be. The concept of separation of church and state is never found in Muslim nations.

"This is eternal life, that they may *know* Thee, the only true God, *and Jesus Christ* whom thou has sent" (Jn. 17:3). Jesus said, "my sheep *know* me" (Jn. 10:14).

The Apostle Paul prayed for Christian believers concerning God, "that you may *know* him better" (Eph. 1:17). The Apostle Paul also said, "I *know* whom I have believed" (2 Tim. 1:12).

The Apostle John emphasized, "We *know* that we have come to *know* him if we obey his commands. The man who says, 'I know him,' but does not do what he commands is a liar, and the truth is not in him" (1 Jn. 2:3-4). Thus, he emphasized, "Dear friends, let us love one another, for love comes from God. Everyone who loves has been born of God and *knows* God. Whoever does not love does not *know* God, because God is love" (1 Jn. 4:7-8).

The above reveals that the Muslim God, Allah, and the biblical God, Yahweh, constitute two distinct and opposing concepts of God. Regrettably, because Muslims teach that Allah alone is the one true God, they claim that Christians worship a false god.

7. *What does Islam teach about Jesus Christ?*

Muslims claim that they believe in the true Jesus Christ. They praise Jesus as a prophet of God, as sinless, as "the Messiah," as "illustrious in this world and the next,"[23] as "the Word of Allah" and as "the Spirit of God." Muslims cite the Koran in confirmation of their belief in Jesus, e.g.: "And we gave Jesus, Son of Mary, the clear signs, and confirmed Him with the Holy Spirit."[24]

Unfortunately, however, Islam does not believe in the *biblical* Jesus. The Bible teaches that Jesus is God's one and only Son. Jesus Himself taught this, e.g., "For God so loved the world that he gave his *one and only Son,* that whoever believes in him shall not perish but have eternal life....Whoever believes in him is not condemned, but whoever does not believe stands condemned already because he has not believed in the name of *God's one and only Son*" (Jn. 3:16,18; cf. Mt. 11:27; 26:64). God Himself declared of Jesus at His baptism, "And a voice from heaven said, 'This is my Son, whom I love; with him I am well pleased' " (Mt. 3:17; cf. 17:5). Finally, the Apostles Paul and John also declared that Jesus is God's Son (Rom 1:3; 1 Jn. 5:9-12). In fact, virtually every book in the New Testament either declares or assumes that Jesus is God's unique Son.

On the other hand, Islam asserts that Jesus was merely one of God's many prophets or messengers, and not God's only Son. Muslims strongly reject the idea that Jesus is the Son of God because the Koran repeatedly emphasizes that Jesus Christ is *not* the literal Son of God:*

> It is not for God to take a son unto Him.[25]

> They say, "God has taken to Him a son."...Say: "Those who forge against God falsehood shall not prosper."[26]

> Praise belongs to God, who has not taken to Him a son....[27]

> ...Warn those who say, "God has taken to Himself a son";...a monstrous word it is, issuing out of their mouths; they say nothing but a lie.[28]

> But who does greater evil than he who forges against God a lie?[29]

> They are unbelievers who say, "God is the Messiah, Mary's Son."[30]

Thus the Koran emphatically denies that Jesus Christ is the Son of God—again, a teaching Jesus Himself just as emphatically affirmed (Jn. 3:16,18; 10:36-38).

In conclusion, the Christian view of Jesus Christ as God's literal Son is considered blasphemous to the Muslim.[31] Ali's translation of Sura 5:73,78 reads, "They do blaspheme who say: 'God is Christ the son of Mary.'... Christ the son of Mary was no more than an apostle."[32]

Obviously, then, Muslims deny that Jesus Christ was God incarnate. Any Muslim who believes that Jesus Christ is God has committed "the one unforgivable sin" called *shirk*—a sin that will send him to hell forever.[33] The Koran clearly teaches that Jesus was only a man: "The Messiah, Jesus Son of Mary, was only the Messenger of God...."[34] Sura 43:59 asserts: "Jesus was no more than a mortal whom [Allah] favored and made an example to the Israelites."[35]

But even though Jesus Himself claimed He *was* God on many different occasions, the Koran rejects this and has Jesus denying His own deity. Thus, when Allah asks Jesus if He is God, Jesus replies, "It is not mine to say

---

* Biblically, Christ's designation as God's Son is a declaration of His deity (Jn. 5:18; 19:7), but Muslims have other objections to Christ being God's Son.

what I have no right to."[36] In fact, even as a baby, Jesus allegedly claimed He was only a servant of Allah. According to Sura 19:20,34, Jesus praised his birth and then said, "I am the servant of Allah."

Further, Muslims do not believe that Jesus was crucified and died on the cross. They believe Allah would never permit this to happen to one of his special prophets.

When Muslims deny that Christ was crucified on the cross—and teach instead that God substituted someone else in His place—they reject the clearest teaching of the New Testament. Even Jesus prophesied—repeatedly—that He had to go to the cross and that this was God's direct will for Him:

> From that time on Jesus began to explain to his disciples that he must go to Jerusalem and suffer many things at the hands of the elders, chief priests and teachers of the law and that he must be killed and on the third day be raised to life (Mt. 16:21).

> Jesus took the Twelve aside and told them, "We are going up to Jerusalem, and everything that is written by the prophets about the Son of Man will be fulfilled. He will be handed over to the Gentiles. They will mock him, insult him, spit on him, flog him and kill him. On the third day he will rise again" (Lk. 18:31-33).

> Now my heart is troubled, and what shall I say? "Father, save me from this hour"? No, it was for this very reason I came to this hour (Jn. 12:27).

Innumerable eyewitnesses, both Jesus' friends and enemies, saw Him die on the cross. Further, many of His apostles and friends were also eyewitnesses to His resurrection from the dead, confirming His claim to be the Son of God (Jn. 19:23-27,31-35; Rom. 1:3).

Finally, Islam teaches that Muhammad was a superior prophet to Jesus because he brought God's final and best revelations to man. Badru D. Kateregga, a former lecturer and head of the Islamic studies and comparative religion at Kenyatta University College, University of Nairobi, Kenya, exemplifies the Muslim view of Jesus as an inferior prophet to Muhammad:

> The truth that all the previous prophets have proclaimed to humanity was perfected by Prophet Muhammad....The Qur'an, which is Allah's *final guidance* to mankind, was revealed to the Prophet Muhammad...the seal of all prophets,

> 600 years after the Prophet Isa (Jesus)…Muhammad…is the
> *one prophet* who fulfilled Allah's mission during his lifetime.

> Muslims believe in and respect all the prophets of God who
> preceded Muhammad….They *all* brought a uniform mes-
> sage—Islam—from Allah. Muhammad is the last in seal of
> prophethood. Through him, Islam was completed and per-
> fected. As he brought the last and latest guidance for all
> mankind, it is *he alone* to whom Muslims turn for guidance.[37]

Thus "Muhammad…is the last prophet and messenger of Allah. His mission was for the whole world and
for all times" (4:35). In other words, Muslims must not
turn to Jesus for spiritual guidance, only to Muhammad.

Again, unfortunately, Muslims are wrong. Jesus
Christ is far more than one of God's messengers or
prophets. As we saw, Jesus Christ is God's one and only
Son (Jn. 3:16-18). Further, He is the Second Person of
the Trinity, God incarnate—God Himself (Jn. 1:1,14;
5:18). Jesus claimed to be both "the Lord" and "God":
"You call me 'Teacher' and 'Lord,' and rightly so, for that
is what I am" (Jn. 13:13). And, "anyone who has seen me
has seen the Father [God]" (Jn. 14:9). "I and the Father
[God] are one" (Jn. 10:30).

In conclusion, both the Koran and the Muslim religion are in error concerning their teachings on the most
important man of history, Jesus Christ. Islam claims
that it honors and reverences Jesus, but it rejects what
the Bible teaches about Him and what He taught about
Himself.

8. *What does Islam teach about salvation?*

Because the Koran teaches that "the true religion
with God is Islam,"[38] this means for the Muslim that salvation is achieved only through submission to the teachings of Allah. Thus, salvation in Islam requires that one
must be a member of the Islamic faith. "Whoso desires
another religion than Islam, it shall not be accepted of
him; in the next world he shall be among the losers."[39]
Thus, "those who disbelieve, and die disbelieving—upon
them shall rest the curse of God and the angels, and of
men altogether, there indwelling forever; the chastisement shall not be lightened for them; no respite shall be
given them."[40]

But what exactly does the Muslim believe about salvation? Here are five basic points that reveal what the religion of Islam teaches about salvation.

A. *Islam teaches that forgiveness is conditioned upon good works and Allah's choice of mercy.*

Islam is a religion of salvation by personal righteousness. In other words, the Muslim thinks that by striving to please God and by doing good works, he will hopefully gain entrance to heaven through personal merit.

The Koran clearly teaches that salvation is achieved on the basis of good works. Consider the following statements:

> ...every soul shall be paid in full what it has earned....[41]

> ...God loves those who cleanse themselves.[42]

> Gardens of Eden, underneath which rivers flow, there indwelling forever; that is the recompense of the self-purified.[43]

Islam teaches that on the Day of Judgment one's good and evil deeds will be weighed on a scale. Good works are heavy and evil deeds are light. Thus the person whose balances are heavy with good deeds will go to heaven, while the person whose scales are light will go to hell. The Koran asserts:

> [In the Day of Judgment] they whose balances shall be heavy with good works, shall be happy; but they whose balances shall be light, are those who shall lose their souls, and shall remain in hell forever.[44]

> With knowledge We will recount to them what they have done, for We are watching over all their actions. On that day, their deeds shall be weighed with justice. Those whose scales are heavy shall triumph, but those whose scales are light shall lose their souls, because they have denied Our revelations.[45]

The Muslim assumes that his chances for heaven are good if he 1) accepts only the Muslim God Allah and his prophet Mohammad, 2) does good works and all that is required of him by Allah (e.g., the Pillars of Religion), and 3) if he is predestined to heaven by Allah's favor.

Given such requirements, one wonders if the Muslim can have any assurance of salvation at all. Abdiyah Akbar Abdul-Haqq comments that the Islamic reliance on good works is bound to leave any Muslim who seeks personal assurance of salvation "utterly confused"[46] because in this life no Muslim can ever know if his good works are finally sufficient—let alone if he is predestined to Allah's favor.

William Miller was a missionary to Muslims in Iran from 1919 to 1962. He discusses the Islamic view of salvation, its dependence upon good works and personal merit, and the uncertainty which this brings to the heart of every Muslim:

> Islam has no Savior. Mohammad is rarely called Savior. He is said to have brought God's laws to men, and they, by keeping those laws, must satisfy God's requirements and win His approval....Since many Muslims realize that they [fall short of Koranic standards]...they recite extra prayers in addition to those required for each day, they make gifts to charity, and go on pilgrimages not only to Mecca, but also to other sacred shrines, in order to gain merit, and if possible, balance their account with God. But since God does not make known how the accounts of His stand, a Muslim facing death does not know whether he is to go to paradise or to hell. After all, the decision is made by the arbitrary will of God, and no one can predict what that decision will be....And so the Muslim lives and dies, not sure of his final salvation.[47]

Thus the Muslim concept of forgiveness is unlike that of biblical Christianity. In biblical Christianity, forgiveness is based upon the death of Christ on the cross as a *past* action. This means that once a person receives Christ as his or her Savior, all of his or her sins are forgiven and each one is *guaranteed* a place in heaven: "I tell you the truth, whoever hears my word and believes him who sent me *has eternal life* and *will not be condemned*" (Jn. 5:24) and "praise be to the God and Father of our Lord Jesus Christ! In his great mercy he has given us new birth into a living hope through the resurrection of Jesus Christ from the dead, and into an inheritance that can *never perish, spoil or fade—kept in heaven for you,* who through faith are shielded by God's power until the coming of the salvation that is ready to be revealed in the last time" (1 Pet. 1:35).

In Islam, there is no atonement for sin—no propitiatory basis for forgiveness of sins. The Bible however, teaches of Jesus, "He is the atoning sacrifice for our sins." Because of His great love for us, Jesus willingly died in our place (see Jn. 10:18), taking the penalty due our sin so that God could freely forgive us. Indeed, "God presented him [Jesus] as a sacrifice of atonement" and

"God did it to demonstrate his justice at the present time, so as to be just and the one who justifies those who have faith in Jesus" (Rom 3:25-26). In Islam, however, Allah simply forgives whom he chooses to forgive. Again, this forgiveness is predicated upon *both* personal merit and Allah's choice of mercy. Muslims never know if their personal works are sufficient to forgive their sins or if Allah will finally be merciful to them. Muslims certainly hope they will be saved. But the following statements in the Koran, as well as others, indicate the conditional nature of Islamic forgiveness:

> ...And whosoever of you turns from his religion, and dies disbelieving—their works have failed in this world and the next; those are the inhabitants of the Fire; therein they shall dwell forever.[48]

> God has pardoned what is past; but whoever offends again, God will take vengeance on him; God is All-mighty, Vengeful.[49]

This is contrary to what the Bible teaches—that full salvation comes solely by God's grace through faith in Jesus Christ, who died for *all* the believers' sins: "He forgave us *all* our sins" (Col. 2:13). The Bible also emphasizes that salvation does not come by good works or anything else we can do to please God on our own efforts: "For we maintain that a man is justified by faith apart from observing the law" (Rom. 3:28). "For it is by grace you have been saved, through faith—and this *not from yourselves,* it is the gift of God—*not by works,* so that no one can boast" (Eph. 2:8-9).

In contrast to the teachings of Islam, the Bible teaches that anyone who wishes may *come* to God, *freely* receive salvation, and *know* he or she is eternally saved. Jesus taught, "For God so loved the world that he gave his one and only Son, that whosoever believes in him shall *not* perish but *have* eternal life" (Jn. 3:16). The Apostle Peter taught, "The Lord...is patient with you, not wanting anyone to perish, but *everyone* to come to repentance" (2 Pet. 3:9). Again, Jesus taught, "He who believes *has* eternal life" (Jn. 6:47) and "I am the Alpha and the Omega, the Beginning and the End. To him who is thirsty I will give to drink *without cost* from the spring of the water of life" (Rev. 21:6). The Apostle John emphasized, "I write these things to you who believe in the name of the Son of God so that you may *know that you have eternal life*" (1 Jn. 5:13).

B. Islam teaches that Jesus Christ was neither crucified nor resurrected; therefore, salvation cannot possibly be had through faith in Christ.

We mentioned earlier that Islam rejects the atoning sacrifice of Christ on the cross. One reason for this is its view that man is basically good; thus, if men are not unredeemed sinners, they do not need a savior from sin, just good works, abstention from wickedness, and Allah's favor. Also, Islam considers Jesus Christ one of Allah's prophets, and it is unthinkable that God would permit one of His prophets to be crucified. Thus, the Muslim religion denies that Christ died upon the cross. The Koran teaches: "They denied the truth and uttered a monstrous falsehood....They declared: 'We have put to death the Messiah, Jesus the son of Mary, the apostle of Allah.' They did not kill him, nor did they crucify him, but they thought they did."[50]

Because Muslims do not believe that Christ died on the cross, they are forced to also deny His resurrection. Ahmad Dedat is one of the leading public defenders of Islam. He claims: "Throughout the length and breadth of the 27 books of the New Testament, there is not a single statement made by Jesus Christ that 'I was dead, and I have come back from the dead.' The Christian has [wrongly] been belaboring the word resurrection. Again and again, by repetition, it is conveyed that it [the resurrection] is proving a fact....[But] Jesus Christ never uttered the word that 'I have come back from the dead,' in the 27 books of the New Testament, not once."[51]

But Mr. Dedat is wrong. On many occasions in the New Testament Jesus predicted both His death *and* His resurrection. For example, He told His disciples, "The Son of Man must suffer many things and be rejected by the elders, chief priests and teachers of the law, and he must be killed *and on the third day be raised to life*" (Lk. 9:22). After His resurrection He told His disciples that this was to fulfill the prophecies written about Him:

> This was what I told you while I was still with you: Everything must be fulfilled that is written about me in the Law of Moses, the Prophets and the Psalms....He told them, "This is what is written: The Christ will suffer and rise from the dead on the third day, and repentance and forgiveness of sins will be preached in his name to all nations..." (Lk. 24:44,46,47).

Further, in Revelation 1:18, Jesus taught, "I am the Living One; *I was dead, and behold I am alive for ever and ever!*"

Muslims also say Jesus Christ will not return at the Second Coming. But in Matthew 16:27; 25:31; and elsewhere, Jesus also predicted His literal, physical return to earth to set up His millennial/eternal kingdom.

Dr. John Elder was missionary to Muslims in Iran from 1922 to 1964. Among his scholarly works are 11 books in Persian and 2 in English. He discusses the Muslim rejection of the atonement and the reasons upon which it is based:

> Like the doctrine of the death of Jesus, the ordinary Muslim completely rejects the doctrine of Jesus' atonement for sin. He rejects it first on [allegedly] historical grounds. If Jesus survived the cross [i.e., never truly died], as the Muslim believes, then He could not have given His life to atone for man's sins.
>
> In the second place, the Muslim idea of God and His decrees recognizes no need for atonement. According to the doctrine of decrees, God determined the fate of all men from the beginning, and we are helpless to change it. This belief is taught in many places in the Qur'an....
>
> A third reason why Muslims deny the possibility of an atonement is their belief that God does not love man, and indeed, is unaffected by man's actions....Any idea that God so loved the world that He gave His only son is completely foreign to the Muslim mind....Thus, a pious Muslim is constantly performing acts which he explains by saying, "savab darad" (it is meritorious). Thus, he saves for most of his lifetime to make the Meccan pilgrimage; he gives money to help erect a mosque; he faithfully reads the Qur'an even though it be in a language he does not understand; and he prays the prescribed Arabic prayers.[52]

In conclusion, Muslims reject the biblical teaching that Christ died for their sins, and, therefore, seek salvation by religious observance. Unfortunately, in doing so they deny their need for Christ and repudiate what Jesus and the Bible teaches concerning His death: "just as the Son of Man did not come to be served, but to serve, and to give his life as a ransom for many" and that "He Himself bore our sins in his body on the Cross, that we might die to sin and live to righteousness..." (Mt. 20:28; 1 Pet. 2:24).

C. The concept of the loving God of the Bible is difficult for the Muslim to accept.

As we have indicated, the God of Islam, Allah, is not ultimately a God of love. In Islam, Allah's "love" is not based on unconditional commitment and self-sacrifice, as is biblical love (1 Cor. 13:1-13). "But God *demonstrates* His own love toward us in that while we were yet sinners Christ died for us" (Romans 5:8). In Islam, Allah's love is based on conditional performance and/or divine decree. In Islamic theology, much like Buddhist philosophy, the concept of love seems is primarily that of "mercy." It is more impersonal than personal.

Dr. J. Christy Wilson observes that the concept of God's love is foreign to Islamic thinking because of the extreme emphasis placed upon Allah's sovereign power and transcendence: "It should be said, however, that most Muslims will misunderstand and question the statement of the New Testament that 'God is love.' His power and sovereign transcendence over all creation are so emphasized in Islam that to call Him a God of love or to address Him as 'Father' would be far from Muslim thought."[53]

John Elder also comments, "In addition to the idea that God does not need men and therefore cannot love, the Muslim commonly cites two main problems in believing that God is love: the existence of sin and pain, and man's insignificance in the vastness of the universe."[54]

But again, the Bible teaches the Islamic view of God is wrong when it declares that "God *is* love" (1 Jn. 4:16).

D. Muslim salvation is fatalistic.

We have discussed the fact that the Muslim concept of forgiveness is conditioned upon good works. On the one hand, we find in the Koran the promise of heaven for those who do good. But on the other hand, the promise is conditional—one must possess the true religion of Islam, obey its precepts, and also find favor with Allah. At this point Islam's salvation (in contrast to that of the Bible) appears to become fatalistic.

The largest apparent indeterminacy in the Muslim concept of salvation is Allah's predestination. The Koran teaches, "All things have we created after a fixed decree...."[55] Further, "God leads astray whomsoever He will; and He guides whomsoever He will...."[56] Abdiyah

Akbar Abdul-Haqq observes: "There are several [Muslim] traditions also about the predestination of all things, including all good and bad actions and guided and misguided people….Even if a person desires to choose God's guidance, he cannot do so without the prior choice of God in favor of his free choice. This is sheer determinism."[57]

Dr. Wilson comments, "The fifth article of [Muslim] faith is predestination…the fact that everything that happens, either good or bad, is foreordained by the unchangeable decrees of Allah. It will be seen at once that this makes Allah the author of evil, a doctrine that most Muslim theologians hold."[58] The Koran teaches, for example, "And if a good thing visits them, they say, 'This is from God'; but if an evil thing visits them, they say, 'This is from thee.' Say: 'Everything is from God.' "[59]

And,

> The man whom Allah guides is rightly guided, but he who is led astray by Allah shall surely be lost. As for those that deny Our revelations, *We have predestined for hell many jinn and many men*….We will lead them step by step to ruin….None can guide the people whom Allah leads astray. He leaves them blundering about in their wickedness….Say: "I have not the power to acquire benefits or to avert evil from myself, except by the will of Allah."[60]

At first glance there does appear to be one way a Muslim can guarantee his salvation. This is found in connection with the Muslim concept of *jihad* or holy war: achieving security of salvation requires death in battle: "If you are slain or die in God's way…it is unto God you shall be mustered…."[61]

> When you meet the unbelievers in the battlefields strike off their heads and, when you have laid them low, bind your captives firmly….Thus shall you do….As for those who are slain in the cause of Allah…he will admit them to the Paradise he has made known to them.[62]

> Allah has given those that fight with their goods and their persons a higher rank than those who stay at home….The unbelievers are your sworn enemies…. Seek out your enemies relentlessly….You shall not plead for traitors….Allah does not love the treacherous or the sinful.[63]

It appears at first that the Muslim is promised heaven for death in battle. But we discover that even this security of salvation is conditioned on something else—in this case, bravery:

> O believers, when you encounter the unbelievers marching to battle, turn not your backs to them. Whoso turns his back that day to them, unless withdrawing to fight again or removing to join another host, he is laden with the burden of God's anger, and his refuge is Gehenna—an evil homecoming![64]

Thus, even in the guarantee of heaven through death in a holy war, the Muslim promise of salvation appears to remain provisional. And none can deny that unnumbered Muslims, trusting in Islam to save them and take them to heaven, have instead been sent to their deaths in the jihads of history and today. They have been sent to eternity without Christ.

E. Do Christians have salvation according to Islam?

Some have claimed that, according to Islam, Christians can remain Christians and still inherit salvation. They also claim that the God of Islam and the God of the Bible are the same God. To the contrary, the Koran teaches that only if Christians convert to Islam and remain good Muslims will they have the opportunity for salvation. If Christians reject the Koran, they are classified as unbelievers and their destiny is an eternal hell:

> God guides not the people of the unbelievers.... They are unbelievers who say, "God is the Messiah, Mary's Son."...The Messiah [Jesus] said, "Children of Israel, serve God, [Allah] my Lord and your Lord. Verily, whoso associates with God anything, God shall prohibit him entrance to Paradise, and his refuge shall be the Fire; and wrong doers shall have no helpers." They are unbelievers who say, "God is the Third of Three." No god is there but One God. If they refrain not from what they say, there shall afflict those of them that disbelieve a painful chastisement....[65]

In the above citation, we see that 1) Christians who believe that Jesus is the divine Messiah are classified as unbelievers; 2) those who believe in the Trinity (that "God is the Third of Three") are unbelievers; and 3) Christians who believe that Christ is God (those who "associate" God with Jesus) will be consigned to hell. Thus, if Christians do not turn from their errors and accept Islam, they are subject to the strictest judgment:

> ...[In war] kill those who join other gods with God [the phrase in other translations reads "kill those who are idolaters,

pagans"] wherever ye shall find them; and seize them, besiege them, and lay wait for them with every kind of ambush: but if they shall convert, and observe prayer, and pay the obligatory alms, then let them go their way, for God is Gracious, Merciful.[66]

Do they not know that whosoever opposes God and His Messenger—for him awaits the fire of Gehenna, therein to dwell forever?[67]

Verily, God will not forgive the union of other gods with Himself!....And He who uniteth gods with God hath devised a great wickedness....The flame of Hell is their sufficing *punishment!* Those who disbelieve our signs we will in the end cast into the fire: so oft as their skins shall be well burnt, we will change them for fresh skins, that they may taste the torment.[68]

Section III
The Bible of Islam:
Is the Koran the Word of God?

9. What does Islam claim about the Koran?

As noted, Islam claims that the Koran is the literal Word of God, dictated supernaturally to Muhammad from the angel Gabriel. Muslims believe the Koran is perfect and without error. Muslims Musa Qutub, Ph.D., and M. Vazir Ali assert that the Koran is the only book ever to "withstand the microscopic and telescopic scrutiny of one and all, without the book stumbling anywhere."[69]

Islam further claims that the teachings of the Koran are in harmony with the autographs of the Bible because this is what the Koran teaches. (Again, it believes Christians have corrupted the Bible so that the Bibles Christians now use are unreliable.)

...and We have sent down to thee the Book [the Koran] with the truth, confirming the Book [the Bible] that was before it, and assuring it.[70]

This Koran could not have been forged apart from God; but it is a *confirmation* of what is before it....[71]

As the *Encyclopedia Britannica* observes, "For the Muslims, the Koran is the Word of God, confirming and consummating earlier revealed books and thereby replacing them...."[72]

10. Does the Koran deny the Bible?

Everyone who carefully and impartially reads both the Bible and the Koran must agree that, as they both stand, the Koran and the Bible contradict one another on every major religious doctrine: the nature of God, Jesus, salvation, man, Scripture, etc. If the New Testament was *not* corrupted, as we will prove, then how could Allah be the inspiration behind *both* the Bible and the Koran, which contradicts it? This would force us to conclude that God's revelations are contradictory—and therefore useless. Consider the following chart, which we documented in Section II:

	The Koran	*The Bible*
God	unitarian	trinitarian
Jesus	a man	God incarnate
Salvation	by works; uncertain	by grace; assured

Again, if the manuscript evidence forces us to conclude the Bible has not been corrupted, there is only one conclusion a Muslim can logically reach. If Allah really inspired *both* the Bible and the Koran, then he contradicts himself to such an extent that it would be impossible to ascertain his teachings or will for men.

Muslims respond by saying that the Bible *has* been corrupted and, therefore, its present teachings are untrustworthy. Only the Koran is pure and uncorrupted. But this argument is indefensible on historic, textual, and even Koranic grounds, as we will see.

In the next 8 questions we will seek to determine if the Koran is "pure and uncorrupted" as Muslims claim, and whether their claim that the Bible is corrupted and untrustworthy is valid.

11. Does the Koran contain historical errors and biblical distortions?

Muslims and Christian agree that it is impossible for God to inspire error in His Word. But no one can deny that the Koran contains a large number of errors. Dr. Robert Morey lists more than 100; e.g., citing Ali's translation, the Koran teaches the Ark of Noah came to rest on the top of Mt. Judi (Sura 11:44), not Mt. Ararat as the Bible teaches; that Abraham's father was Azar (Sura 6:74), not Terah as the Bible teaches; that he attempted to sacrifice Ishmael (Sura 37:100-112), not

Isaac as the Bible teaches; that Pharaoh's *wife* adopted Moses (Sura 28:8-9), not his daughter as the Bible teaches; that Noah's flood occurred in Moses' day (Sura 7:136, cf., 7:59ff.); that Mary, the mother of Jesus, gave birth to Jesus under a palm tree (Sura 19:22), not in a stable as the Bible teaches; that Mary's father was named Imram (Sura 66:12), etc.[73]

In the preface to his translation of the Koran, Rodwell notes the presence of "contradictory and...inaccurate statements."[74] For example, Muhammad is nowhere found in the Bible, but the Koran claims that Muhammad himself is "described in the Torah and the Gospel."[75] The disciples of Christ were obviously Christians, but the Koran teaches that the disciples of Christ were Muslims. Six hundred years before Muhammad was born, Christ's disciples allegedly claim, "We believe; and bear thou witness that we are Muslims."[76]

The Koran also teaches that Abraham was not a Jew but a Muslim. "No; Abraham in truth was not a Jew, neither a Christian; but he was a Muslim...."[77] But the Jews consider Abraham a Jew. The Christians consider Abraham a Jew. Jesus Himself considered Abraham a Jew. All the world considers Abraham a Jew—except the Koran.

There are also some rather unlikely events in the Koran. For example, after Allah tempts the people to sin in judgment for their evil, "when they had scornfully persisted in what they had been forbidden, We changed them into detested apes."[78] According to history, the army of the king of Ethiopia, Abraha, halted its attack on Mecca due to a smallpox outbreak. But Sura 105 teaches he was defeated by birds that dropped stones of baked clay on the soldiers.

Finally, the Koran has many biblical distortions.[79] Almost every biblical episode discussed in the Koran has additional and/or contrary information supplied: "The names and events of Old Testament books and prophets are very definitely copied in the Quran. However, often the stories in the Quran are garbled and confused."[80] For example, in Sura 2:56,57,61 the Jews returned to Egypt *after* the Exodus which, biblically and historically, was never the case. In Sura 3:41 it is stated that Zechariah would be speechless for *three days*. Biblically, it was until John's birth—nine *months* (Lk. 1:18-20). In Sura 12:11-20 the Koranic story of Joseph is markedly different from the biblical story of Genesis 37; the accounts are so contrary as to demand one be in error. In Sura 2:241 Muhammad confuses the persons of Saul and Gideon. There are also variations in Sura 12:21-32, 36-55 when compared with Genesis 37–45.[81]

Whether it is the descriptions of the creation of man, the Fall, Moses and the burning bush, Noah and the ark, Joseph going into Egypt, or the lives of Zechariah, John the Baptist, Mary and Jesus, or other biblical characters, the Koran often contradicts biblical teaching.[82]

Yet the Koran also explicitly claims to "confirm the Book of Moses and the Gospel."[83] So if the Bible is historically accurate, then it is the Koran that must be in error.

12. Does the Koran contain contradictory teachings?

The Koran claims that it contains no contradictions. In Sura 4:84 Allah challenges men, "Will they not ponder on the Koran? If it had not come from Allah, they could have surely found in it many contradictions."[84] Since Allah claims not to contradict himself, then everything that has purportedly "come down from him" (the Bible, the Koran) must be in agreement. The Muslim must believe in the doctrinal unity among the books of Allah—the Bible as originally given and the Koran. But we have just seen they conflict; further, the Koran contains contradictions within its own pages. In Sura 11 the Koran teaches that one of Noah's sons didn't go into the ark and thus "Noah's son was drowned" in the Flood.[85] The Koran itself contradicts this statement in Sura 21, where it declares that "we saved him [Noah] and *all* his kinsfolk from the great calamity...."[86] According to the Bible, all of Noah's sons are delivered (Gen. 6, 7) and the genealogies are provided.

The Koran also has conflicting accounts of Muhammad's original call to be a prophet in Sura 53:2-18; 81:19-24 vs. Sura 16:102; 26:192-94 vs. Sura 15:18; 2:97.

Sura 41:9-12 teaches it took God eight days to create the world, whereas Sura 7:51; 10:3; and 11:6 teach it took God six days. (For more examples, see *Islamic Invasion* by Robert Morey.)

Section IV
Islam: A General Critique

13. How convincing are Muslim apologetics?

The word apologetics is derived from the Greek *apologia*, which means "to present a defense for."

In "How Muslims Do Apologetics," philosopher and theologian John Warwick Montgomery discusses a characteristic problem of Muslim apologetics—that of defending Islam by "discrediting" Christianity. But "such refutations are not 'apologies' or defenses at all, but are *ad hominem* arguments of an offensive nature."[87] Even if Muslim apologists *could* disprove Christianity, this would not prove the truth of Islam. Islam would still require—on its own merits—independent verification as a revelation of God. And because the evidence is lacking, it is precisely at this point that Muslim apologists fail. Muhammad was clearly inspired by some supernatural source, but how could he be inspired by God if his inspiration rejected God's revelation in the Bible?

Biblical inspiration and accuracy are independently verified by prophecy, archeology, manuscript evidence, and other means. We have documented this in some detail in our book *Ready with an Answer* (Harvest House, 1997). Islam, however, offers no genuine evidence for its claim that the Koran is inspired, other than Muhammad's own claim he was inspired by Gabriel. But what if Muhammad was wrong? If the biblical God is the true God and if Muhammad were a prophet of God, he would never have denied God's revelation in the Bible.

So how do Muslims do apologetics? First, they argue that the Christian faith is a false religion. Specifically, using the arguments of liberal theologians, higher critical methods (e.g., form criticism), and rationalistic skeptics of Christianity, they reject biblical authority and the deity of Christ.[88] Second, they present arguments in defense of Islam that are convincing to Muslims but are also largely subjective and prove nothing.[89] In essence, Muslim apologetics are not convincing because they characteristically reject the rules of logic and evidence. Space does not permit elaboration, except to refer the reader to taped sessions of Christian–Muslim debates and more specific evaluations of Muslim apologetic methods. For illustrations we would recommend first, the 7-hour debate between Dr. Robert A. Morey and Dr.

Jamal Badawi, who some Muslims claim is the best apologist for Islam in North America. Second, we would recommend other materials published by both Muslims and Christians.[90] In essence, after evaluating Muslim apologetics we are forced to conclude that the average Muslim, unknowingly and regrettably, has been misled by apologists whose primary arguments are based on subjectivism, logical fallacies, anachronism, and unfortunate historical errors.

14. What basic problem does the Koran present to Muslims?

As we have indicated, the Koran teaches that Muslims are to accept *both* the Bible and the Koran:

> Say: "We believe in God, and that which has been sent down on us, and sent down on Abraham and Ishmael, Isaac and Jacob, and the [Jewish] Tribes, and in that which was given to Moses and Jesus, and the Prophets, of their Lord; *we make no division between any of them....*"[91]

The Koran claims that *Allah* is the God who inspired the Old Testament and the New Testament: "...We gave to Moses the Book and the Salvation, that haply you should be guided."[92] Muslims are commanded, "Observe the Torah and the Gospel...what is revealed to them from Allah."[93]

Elsewhere Muslims are told:

> O believers, believe in God and His Messenger [Muhammad] and the Book He has sent down on His Messenger [the Koran] and the Book which He sent down before [the Bible]. Whoso disbelieves in God and His angels and His Books, and His Messengers, and the Last Day, has surely gone astray into far error....God will gather the hypocrites and the unbelievers all in Gehenna.[94]

In the above verses we see that those who *reject* God's Books (plural) and Messengers (plural) are said to be unbelievers![95] Muslims are thus forbidden by Allah to accept only part of God's revelations. But here is a keen dilemma. If Muslims accept what the Koran teaches, they must then accept what the Bible teaches—which rejects what the Koran teaches.

But if a Muslim truly accepts the Bible and rejects what the Koran teaches, he can no longer remain a Muslim and should become a Christian.[96] So how can a Muslim trust what the Koran teaches when it simultaneously undermines its own authority? How does the Muslim circumvent this difficulty? By claiming the Bible's teachings have been corrupted and are therefore untrustworthy.

15. Is the Muslim claim that the Bible has been corrupted based on facts or bias?

The Koran and Islam claim that the Bible has been corrupted by Christians: "People of the Book [Jews and Christians], now there has come to you Our Messenger [Muhammad], making clear to you many things you have been concealing of the Book, and defacing many things."[97]

In his *Christian Faith and Other Faiths*, Oxford theologian Stephen Neill observes:

> It is well known that at many points the Qur'an does not agree with the Jews and Christian Scriptures. Therefore, from the Muslim point of view, it follows of necessity that these Scriptures must have been corrupted. Historical evidence makes no impression on the crushing force of the syllogism. So it is, and it can be no other way. The Muslim controversialist feels no need to study evidence in detail. The only valid picture of Jesus Christ is that which is to be found in the pages of the Qur'an.[98]

In other words, because the Koran is predefined as God's perfect revelation and the Bible contradicts it, the Bible must be corrupted. Historical evidence has no relevance to the issue because it is impossible that the Koran could be wrong.[99]

But this is placing the cart before the horse. One must first determine if the Bible was corrupted. If not, then the error must lie with the Koran. And historical facts prove that the Bible has not been corrupted.[100] If Muslims refuse to honestly examine and accept this evidence, it is hardly the fault of Christians.

For example, after a thorough evaluation of the textual evidence and citing numerous scholars in confirmation, Drs. Geisler and Nix conclude that a modern critical edition of the Bible says "exactly what the autographs contained—line for line, word for word, and even letter for letter."[101] Therefore, for the Muslim to maintain that the Bible has been corrupted is an indefensible position. (We discuss this in greater detail in Q. 18.)

16. Is the Koran uncorrupted?

Historical facts prove that it is the Koran that has been corrupted. First, the Koran is not written in perfect Arabic (cf. Sura 12:2; 13:37; 41:41,44) but has scores of grammatical errors and non-Arabic words.[102] Second, the text of the Koran itself has been corrupted:

> There are many conflicting readings on the text of the Quran as Arthur Jeffrey has demonstrated in his book *Material for the History of the Text of the Quran.* At one point, Jeffrey gives 90 pages of variant readings on the text. For example, in Sura 2 there are over 140 conflicting and variant readings....

> All Western and Muslim scholars admit the presence of variant readings in the text of the Quran. Guillaume points out that the Quran at first "had a large number of variants, not always trifling in significance."...The work of Western scholars such as Arthur Jeffrey and others has been hampered by Muslim reluctance to let Western scholars see old manuscripts of the Quran which are based on pre-Uthman texts....According to Professor Guillaume in his book *Islam* (pp. 191ff.), some of the original verses of the Quran were lost. For example, one Sura originally had 200 verses in the days of Ayesha. But by the time Uthman standardized the text of the Quran, it had only 73 verses! A total of 127 verses had been lost, and they have never been recovered. The Shiite Muslims claim that Uthman left out 25 percent of the original verses in the Quran for political reasons.

> That there are verses which got left out of Uthman's version of the Quran is universally recognized. John Burton's book, *The Collection of the Quran,* which was published by Cambridge University, documents how such verses were lost. Burton states concerning the Muslim claim that the Quran is perfect: "The Muslim accounts of the history of the Quran texts are a mass of confusion, contradictions and inconsistencies...."

> In the abrogation process spoken of earlier [referring to the Quran], verses which are contradictory to Muslim faith and practice have been removed from the text, such as the "satanic verses" in which Muhammad approved of the worship of the three goddesses, the daughters of Allah....Not only have parts of the Quran been lost, but entire verses and chapters have been added to it. For example, Ubai had several Suras in his manuscript of the Quran which Uthman omitted from his standardized text. Thus there were Qurans in circulation before Uthman's text which had additional revelations from Muhammad that Uthman did not find or approve of, and thus he failed to place them in his text....Western scholars have shown beyond reasonable doubt that Uthman's text did not

contain all of the Quran. Neither was what it did contain correct in all of its wording….The true history of the collection and the creation of the text of the Quran reveals that the Muslim claims are indeed fictitious and not in accord with the facts.[103]

Thus, even the *earliest* copies of the Koran must have contradicted one another or had other problems. Why? Because these copies "led to such serious disputes between the faithful" that it was necessary "to establish a text which should be the sole standard."[104] Dr. William Miller reveals that "for some years after the death of Muhammad there was *great confusion* as to what material of all that had been preserved should be included in the Koran. Finally, in the caliphate of Uthman (644–656 A.D.) one text was given official approval, and all [other] material was destroyed."[105]

For Muslims to have destroyed such materials, the earlier versions of the Koran must have differed significantly from this official version:

The recording of the prophet's words in the beginning was haphazard. Verses were written on palm leaves, stones, the shoulder-blades of animals—in short, on any material which was available….Before an authorized version was established under the caliph Uthman there were four rival editions in use. These have long since disappeared, but we are told that they differed from the authorized version….[106]

On account of the variations and confusions which had arisen among the reported sayings of Mohammed…a revision [was] made, and all existing copies of the previous compilation [were] destroyed. Thus, the present text of the Koran is not the first edition, but a second edition….[107]

But how accurate were the written messages or the memories of those who first heard the prophet? Were the diverse sources from which the Koran was compiled equally reliable? If so, why destroy them? Did Muhammad ever claim inspiration even when he was not inspired? Also, we have already seen that the revelations were tampered with. In this regard, respected Muslim authority Guillaume further comments that "the Quran as we have it now is a record of what Muhammad said while in the [seizure] state or states just mentioned. It is beyond doubt that his hearers recognized the symptoms of revelation…. [However,] one of the secretaries he employed boasted that he had induced the prophet to alter the wording of the revelations."[108]

Muslims may claim that the Arabic Koran is the same today as when it was first given to Muhammad, but this is not true. In *The Islam Debate*, Josh McDowell comments:

> The Quran's transmission is not free from errors and variant readings in significant points. There is concrete evidence in the best works of Islamic tradition (e.g., *Sahih of Muslim*, the *Sahih of Bukhari*, the *Mishkat-ul-Masabih*), that from the start the Qur'an had numerous variant and conflicting readings. That these are no longer found in the Quran is only because they have been discreetly removed—not by direction of God, but by human discretion. There is similar evidence that, to this day, verses and, indeed, whole passages are still missing from the Qur'an.[109]

Dr. Anis Shorrosh, a Christian Arab, concludes his own study of the Koran with:

> It is not the Bible which is contradictory and confusing. No, it is definitely the Quran. If Muslims insist that the Bible is corrupt, I will have to declare that the evidence, much of which I have presented in this book, vindicates the Bible and condemns the Quran. No reasonable person presented with the evidence can believe otherwise.[110]

In conclusion, Muslims have never proven that the Bible has been corrupted. But sufficient evidence exists to show the Koran was.

17. Can the Koran be objectively interpreted?

Dr. J. Christy Wilson comments about the problems of interpreting the Koran:

> It is most difficult for one who is not a Muslim to understand the theory that the Koran was inscribed from all eternity on a tablet in heaven, because some verses supersede and cancel others....Even to Muslims much of the text is unintelligible except through a commentary....It is kept with the utmost reverence, only touched after ceremonial ablutions, and read or recited by many millions of Muslims who do not understand the meaning of its Arabic verses.[111]

In the introduction to his translation, Dawood comments that because the Koran was originally written in the Kufic script and there was, therefore, no indication of vowels or diacritical points, "variant readings are recognized by Muslims as of equal authority" and "it ought to be borne in mind that the Koran contains many statements which, if not recognized as altogether obscure, lend themselves to more than one interpretation."[112]

In Sura 2:100 the Koran itself teaches, "And for whatever verse We abrogate or cast into oblivion, We bring a better or the like of it; knowest thou not that God is powerful over everything?"[113]

This verse may serve the Muslim as a rationale for contradictions between the Koran and the Bible or the Koran and itself, but what does it say about Allah and His ability to communicate His Word clearly and effectively? Nowhere in the Koran does Allah identify those verses he has repealed or destroyed. How then does the Muslim know which verses are legitimate—and which are not?

Even the Koran teaches that its ambiguous parts are incapable of interpretation:

> It is He who sent down upon thee the Book, wherein are verses clear that are the Essence of the Book, and others ambiguous. As for those in whose hearts is swerving, they follow the ambiguous part, desiring dissension, and desiring its interpretation; and none knows its interpretation, save only God. And those firmly rooted in knowledge say, "We believe in it; all is from our Lord"; yet none remembers, but men possessed of minds.[114]

Here we are told the clear verses are the *essence* of the Koran. If so, one could assume Muslims would rarely disagree as to the interpretation of the clear parts. Is this what we find historically or today? Unfortunately no. Have Muslims ever identified which are the "clear" parts and which are the "ambiguous" parts? If much of the Koran is to varying degrees unclear, on what objective basis can one determine its meaning? And if the material is unessential, why record or reveal it in the first place? Also, how does the Muslim know all that is involved in having a swerving heart or how this relates to knowing the location of the ambiguous parts? The Koran also claims, "Those who have been given the Book know it is the truth from their Lord...."[115] But in light of what we have discussed so far, upon what *objective* basis can a Muslim know this?

As we saw, the Koran teaches that Allah occasionally changes his mind concerning the validity of his word.

Here and there one verse is changed for another. But when critics pointed this out and charged Muhammad with tampering, they themselves were charged with ignorance. "And when We exchange a verse in the place of another verse—and God knows very well what He is sending down—they say, 'Thou art a mere forger!' Nay, but the most of them have no knowledge."[116] Another translation reads, "When We change one verse for another (Allah knows best what He reveals), they say: 'You are an impostor.' Indeed, most of them are ignorant men."[117]

Allah may know best what he reveals, but again, how are mortals to sort out the meaning? How does a Muslim decide which verse is "exchanged" or now preferred by Allah? Further, why would Allah exchange one verse in place of another verse? Why wouldn't he speak clearly the first time?

These are more than mere academic issues. Muslims trust in the Koran for their eternal salvation. But if Muslims are uncertain of what God says—and of His intention—how can they know God's will for their lives? How can they find salvation? By contrast, both Christians and Muslims can know exactly what Jesus Christ taught because His words have never been changed or corrupted. In our final question we will see why.

Section V
The Accuracy of the New Testament Text

18. Can it be proved that the New Testament text is historically reliable and accurate?

Christians and skeptical non-Christians, including Muslims and members of religious cults like Mormonism, have different views concerning the credibility of the Gospels and the rest of the New Testament (NT). For the Christian, nothing is more vital than the very words of Jesus Himself who promised, "Heaven and earth will pass away, but my words will never pass away" (Mt. 24:35). Jesus' promise is of no small import. In other words, if His words were *not* accurately recorded in the Gospels, how can anyone know what He really taught? The truth is, we couldn't know. Further, if the remainder of the New Testament cannot be established to be historically reliable, then little if anything can be known about what true Christianity really is, teaches, or means.

Christians maintain that anyone who wishes can prove to their own satisfaction that, on the basis of accepted bibliographic, internal, external, and other criteria, the New Testament text can be established to be reliable. Textually, we know we have over 99% of the autographs (the remaining 1% is found in variant readings) and there is simply no legitimate basis upon which to doubt the credibility and accuracy of the New Testament writers. No Christian doctrine or moral teaching rests upon a variant reading, the vast majority of which are insignificant. Further, the methods used by the critics that Muslims so often rely on (rationalist, higher critical methods) which claim "assured results" proving the NT unreliable, have been weighed in the balance of *secular* scholarship and found wanting. Their use in biblical analysis is therefore unjustified. Even in a positive sense relative to the biblical text, the fruit these methods have born is miniscule while, negatively, they are responsible for a tremendous weight of destruction relative to people's confusion over biblical authority and their confidence in the Bible. And even fair-minded biblical critics would have to agree that higher criticism's 200-year failure to prove its case, by default strengthens the conservative Christian view as to biblical inspiration and reliability.

In this sense, the critics who continue to advance discredited theories relative to the NT conform to the warnings of Chauncey Sanders in his *Introduction to Research in English Literary History*. He warns literary critics to be certain they are also careful to examine the evidence *against* their case: "He must be as careful to collect evidence against his theory as for it. It may go against the grain to be very assiduous in searching for ammunition to destroy one's own case; but it must be remembered that the overlooking of a single detail may be fatal to one's whole argument. Moreover, it is the business of the scholar to seek the truth, and the satisfaction of having found it should be ample recompense for having to give up a cherished but untenable theory."[118]

In order to resolve this issue of NT reliability for the fair-minded Muslim or skeptic, each should recognize that the following ten facts cannot logically be denied.

Fact One

The existence of 5,300 Greek manuscripts (mss.) and portions, 10,000 Latin Vulgate and 9,300 other versions, along with the papyri mss. and early uncial mss. dating much closer to the original than for any other ancient literature proves the NT has not been corrupted.

Fact Two

The lack of proven fraud or error on the part of *any* New Testament author generally shows the writers were trustworthy in what they wrote.

Fact Three

The writings of reliable Christian sources outside the New Testament also confirm its integrity.

Fact Four

The existence of a number of Jewish and secular accounts about Jesus confirm several basic NT teachings.

Fact Five

Detailed archeological data concerning the New Testament proves the authors wrote with care and accuracy.

Fact Six

The many powerful first-century enemies of Jesus and the apostolic church would have proven fraud or pointed out other problems if they could, but they never did.

Fact Seven

The presence of numerous credible living eyewitnesses to the events recorded, especially of Jesus' death and resurrection, offers powerful evidence as to the truth of what was recorded.

Fact Eight

There are positive appraisals by conservative and even some liberal authorities bearing on the issue of the genuineness of traditional authorship and the early date of the New Testament books, further confirming their integrity.

Fact Nine

There are consistent scholarly, factual reversals of the negative conclusions of higher criticism which undermine its own foundations and credibility.

Fact Ten

There is powerful legal and other testimony as to New Testament reliability.

We have discussed each of these points and provided documentation in our *Ready with an Answer* and *The Facts on the Reliability of the Bible* (Harvest House, 1997). These facts demonstrate the accuracy and reliability of the New Testament behind reasonable doubt. Unfortunately, space permits citing only one of the previous ten points.

Fact Ten—corroboration from legal testimony and former skeptics

We must concede the historicity of the NT when we consider that many great minds of legal history have, on the grounds of strict legal evidence alone, accepted the New Testament as reliable history—not to mention that many skeptical intellects have converted to Christianity on the basis of the historical evidence (Saul of Tarsus, Athanagoras, Augustine, George Lyttleton and Gilbert West, C.S. Lewis, Frank Morison, Sir William Ramsay, John Warwick Montgomery, etc.).

Lawyers, of course, are expertly trained in the matter of evaluating evidence and are perhaps the most qualified in the task of weighing data critically. Is it coincidence that so many of them throughout history have concluded in favor of the truth of the Christian religion? What of the "father of international law," Hugo Grotius, who wrote *The Truth of the Christian Religion* (1627)? Or the greatest authority in English and American common-law evidence in the nineteenth century, Harvard Law School professor Simon Greenleaf, who wrote *Testimony of the Evangelists*, in which he powerfully demonstrated the reliability of the gospels?[119] What of Edmund H. Bennett (1824–1898), for over 20 years the dean of Boston University Law School, who penned *The Four Gospels from a Lawyer's Standpoint* (1899)?[120] What of Irwin Linton, who in his time had represented cases before the Supreme Court

and wrote *A Lawyer Examines the Bible* (1943, 1977), in which he stated:

> So invariable had been my observation that he who does not accept wholeheartedly the evangelical, conservative belief in Christ and the Scriptures has never read, has forgotten, or never been able to weigh—and certainly is utterly unable to refute—the irresistible force of the cumulative evidence upon which such faith rests, that there seems ample ground for the conclusion that such ignorance is an invariable element in such unbelief. And this is so even though the unbeliever be a preacher, who is supposed to know this subject if he know no other.[121]

What of hundreds of contemporary lawyers who, also on the grounds of strict legal evidence, accept the NT as historically accurate? The eminent Lord Chancellor Hailsham has twice held the highest office possible for a lawyer in England, that of Lord Chancellor. He wrote, e.g., *The Door Wherein I Went*, in which he upholds the truth of the Christian Religion. What of Jacques Ellul or of Sir Norman Anderson, one of the greatest authorities on Islamic law, who is a Christian convinced of NT authority and reliability?

Certainly such men are well-acquainted with legal reasoning and have just as certainly concluded that the evidence for the historic truthfulness of the Scriptures is beyond reasonable doubt. As apologist, theologian, and lawyer John W. Montgomery observes in *The Law Above the Law* considering the "ancient documents" rule (that ancient documents constitute competent evidence if there is no evidence of tampering and they have been accurately transmitted); the "parol evidence" rule (Scripture must interpret itself without foreign intervention); the "hearsay rule" (the demand for primary-source evidence); and the "cross examination" principle (the inability of the enemies of Christianity to disprove its central claim that Christ resurrected bodily from the dead in spite of the motive and opportunity to do so)—all these coalesce directly or indirectly to support the preponderance of evidence for Christianity while the burden of proof proper (the legal burden) for disproving it rests with the critic, who, in 2,000 years, has yet to prove his case.[122]

We must, then, emphasize that to reject the New Testament accounts as true history is, by definition, to reject the canons of legitimate historical study. To reject the Gospels or the New Testament is to reject primary historical documentation in general. If this cannot be done, the NT must be retained as careful historical reporting. The NT has proven itself reliable in the crucible of history. It is the NT *critic* who has been unable to prove his case. Nor are the implications small. Legal scholar J.N.D. Anderson observes in *Christianity: The Witness of History:*

> ...It seems to me inescapable that anyone who chanced to read the pages of the New Testament for the first time would come away with one overwhelming impression—that here is a faith firmly rooted in certain allegedly historical events, a faith which would be false and misleading if those events had not actually taken place, but which, if they did take place, is unique in its relevance and exclusive in its demands on our allegiance. For these events did not merely set a "process in motion and then themselves sink back into the past. The unique historical origin of Christianity is ascribed permanent, authoritative, absolute significance; what happened once is said to have happened once for all and therefore to have continuous efficacy."[123]

In essence, the Muslim claim that the NT has been corrupted textually is not only untrue, it can never be substantiated due to the nature of the textual and other evidence at hand. Simply put, facts are facts.

As for the Muslim claim that Christians have so severely misinterpreted their own Scriptures that they teach a false view of God, Jesus, salvation, etc., one must remember that we have had almost 2,000 years of universally accepted Christian doctrine—doctrine that even skeptics of Christianity freely confess the Bible teaches. This is why anyone who wishes can determine the basic doctrine of the NT just by studying it.

In conclusion, Muslim claims relative to the NT are simply not credible. We can only trust that, as some Muslims have done in every generation since Islam was founded, Muslims today will impartially investigate the evidence for New Testament authenticity, and, hopefully, that they will respond accordingly.

19. What can Muslims do who desire to know that they have eternal life?

If you are a Muslim who is willing to accept the evidence and who desires to *know* that you have eternal life, what can you do? Jesus promises that all who believe on Him can know that they *now* possess eternal life: "This is eternal life, that they may *know* Thee, the only true God, and Jesus Christ whom thou has sent" (Jn. 17:3). "Truly, truly, I say to you, he who believes *has eternal life*" (Jn. 6:47). "I tell you the truth, whoever hears my word and believes him who sent me *has eternal life* and will not be condemned; he has *crossed over* from death to life" (Jn. 5:24); "My sheep listen to my voice; I know them, and they follow me. *I give them eternal life,* and they shall *never perish;* no one can snatch them out of my hand" (Jn. 10:27-28).

If you have longed for a personal relationship with God, a relationship in which you know that God loves you, and yet have been unable to find this in Islam, then the true God offers you this opportunity. God tells us that "all have sinned and fall short of the glory of God" (Rom. 3:23). God has promised us full forgiveness of sins (Heb. 10:14) if we turn from our sin and turn to Christ, believing on Him for salvation: "For the wages of sin is death, but the gift of God is eternal life in Christ Jesus our Lord" (Rom. 6:23):

> For God so loved the world that he gave his one and only Son, that whoever believes in him shall not perish but have eternal life. For God did not send his Son into the world to condemn the world, but to save the world through him. Whoever believes in him is not condemned, but whoever does not believe stands condemned already because he has not believed in the name of God's one and only Son (Jn. 3:16-18).

And,

> We accept man's testimony, but God's testimony is greater because it is the testimony of God, which he has given about his Son. Anyone who believes in the Son of God has this testimony in his heart. Anyone who does not believe God has made him out to be a liar, because he has not believed the testimony God has given about his Son. And this is the testimony: God has given us eternal life, and this life is in his Son. He who has the Son has life; he who does not have the Son of God does not have life. I write these things to you who believe in the name of the Son of God so that you may know that you have eternal life (1 Jn. 5:9-13).

If you sincerely desire to know God personally, to know that your sins are forgiven—and that a place in heaven *is* reserved for you (1 Pet. 1:4-5), you can know

44

this by praying the following prayer to receive Jesus Christ as your personal Lord and Savior:

> Dear God:
>
> I acknowledge my sinfulness before You. I confess that I have been trying to earn my own salvation by following the teachings of the Koran. But I now realize that Allah is not the true God. I recognize my need for forgiveness and now realize that Christ died for my sins on the cross. I now receive Him as my personal Savior and Lord. Give me courage and strength to face the opposition I may encounter. Help me to lead others to You as well. In Jesus' name I pray. Amen.

If you have prayed this prayer, please write us at "The John Ankerberg Show" so we may send you some helpful materials about growing in the Christian life. We also recommend that you begin to read the New Testament to know more about the true Jesus Christ. In addition, attend a church that honors Christ as Lord and the Bible as God's Word. Talk to God daily in prayer. The following books will help you grow in the Christian life: 1) J.I. Packer, *God's Words* (InterVarsity); 2) Francis Schaeffer, *True Spirituality* (Tyndale); 3) Abdiyah Akbar Abdul-Haqq, *Sharing Your Faith with a Muslim* (Bethany); 4) William Miller, *Ten Muslims Meet Christ* (Eerdmans); and 5) Mark Hannah, *The True Path: Seven Muslims Make Their Greatest Discovery* (International Doorways).

NOTES

Note to reader: Sura references are taken either from the Arberry, Rodwell, Dawood, or Ali translations. Translators differ somewhat in their numbering of verses; verses may be off by two or three, or paragraphs may be numbered rather than verses. Some translations do not number either verses or paragraphs. Chapters are also numbered differently in English and Arabic. Starred books are recommended reading. See also C.R. Marsh, *Sharing Your Faith with a Muslim* (Moody) and North Africa Mission, *Reaching Muslims Today: A Short Handbook*. Additional important materials are available from 1) Reach Out, Box 18478, Boulder, CO 80308-8478; 2) California Institute of Apologetics (formerly Truth Seekers); 3) Fellowship of Faith for the Muslims, 205 Yonge Street, Room 25, Toronto, Ontario M5B 1N4, Canada; 4) The Samuel Zwemer Institute, Box 365, Altadena, CA 91001; 5) North Africa Mission, 239 Fairfield Avenue, Upper Darby, PA 19082; 6) Africa Christian Press, 16 Morwell Street, London WCIB 3AP, England; 7) The U.S. Center for World Missions, 1605 Elizabeth Street, Pasadena, CA 91104.

1. Sir Norman Anderson, ed., *The World's Religions* (Downer's Grove, IL: InterVarsity, 1976, rev.), p. 91.

2. J. Christy Wilson, *Introducing Islam* (New York: Friendship Press, 1965, rev.), p. 30.

3. A.J. Arberry, *The Koran Interpreted* (New York: MacMillan, 1976), cover statement.

4. C. George Fry and James R. King, *Islam: A Survey of the Muslim Faith* (Grand Rapids: Baker, 1981), p. 38.

5. Stephen Neill, *Christian Faith and Other Faiths* (Downer's Grove, IL: InterVarsity, 1984), p. 63.

6. Robert A. Morey, *Islamic Invasion* (Eugene, OR: Harvest House, 1992), p. 175.

7. Walter R. Martin, "The Black Muslim Cult," in *The Kingdom of the Cults,* (Minneapolis: Bethany, 1970 ed.), pp. 259-75.

* 8. Morey, *Islamic Invasion,* pp. 21-23; other materials from the organizations cited in the "Note to reader." See also John Ankerberg and John Weldon, *One World: Bible Prophecy and the New World Order* (Chicago: Moody Press, 1991), pp. 110-20; see Notes 9 and 10.

9. Ibid.

10. Anis A. Shorrosh, *Islam Revealed: A Christian Arab's View of Islam* (Nashville: Nelson, 1998), p. 172; Uzra Zeya, "Muslims in America Face Educational Challenges," *Reach Out,* vol. 4, nos. 3 & 4, Fall/Winter 1990, p. 18; and "Countries with a Significant Muslim Population," pp. 12-13; Dave Hunt, *CIB Bulletin,* PO Box 7349, Bend, OR 97708, April 1991.

11. A.M. Holt, ed., *The Cambridge History of Islam,* vol. 2 (London: Cambridge University Press, 1970), cited in Josh McDowell and John Gilchrist, *The Islam Debate* (San Bernardino, CA: Here's Life Publishers, 1983), p. 16.

12. J.N.D. Anderson, ed., *The World's Religions* (Grand Rapids: Eerdmans, 1966), pp. 54, 60; see also Morey, pp. 69-88, 93-99.

13. Robert Payne, *The Holy Sword* (New York: Collier, 1962), cited in Josh McDowell and John Gilchrist, *The Islam Debate* (San Bernardino, CA: Here's Life Publishers, 1983), p. 15.

14. John Elder, *The Biblical Approach to the Muslim* (Fort Washington, PA: Worldwide Evangelization Crusade, 1978), pp. 30-31; McDowell and Gilchrist, *Debate,* p. 19 passim.

15. Arberry, p. 15.

16. Ibid., p. 65.

17. Ibid., p. 140.

18. Ibid., pp. 139-40.

19. See our *Knowing the Truth About the Trinity* (Eugene, OR: Harvest House, 1997). Also see E. Calvin Beisner, *God in Three Persons* (Wheaton, IL: Tyndale, 1984) and Edward Bickersteth, *The Trinity* (Grand Rapids, MI: Kregel, rpt.).

20. E.g., Arberry, pp. 81, 90, 142, 178, 204.

21. Cited in a book review in *Reach Out,* vol. 6, nos. 3 & 4, 1993, p. 15.

22. George Houssney, "What Is Allah Like?" *Reach Out,* vol. 6, nos. 3 & 4, 1993, pp. 12-13.

23. E.g., Sura 3:45.

24. Arberry, p. 64.

25. N.J. Dawood, *The Koran* (Baltimore: Penguin Books, 1972), p. 34.

26. Ibid., p. 233.

27. Ibid., p. 315.

28. Ibid., p. 316.

29. Ibid., p. 317.

30. Ibid., p. 130.

46

*31. J.N.D. Anderson, *Christianity and Comparative Religion* (Downer's Grove, IL: InterVarsity, 1970 ed.), p. 47.

32. A. Yusuf Ali, *The Holy Qur'an* (Washington, D.C.: The Islamic Center, 1978), p. 266.

33. *Tawhid* is the doctrine of the singularity of Allah; *shirk* is its opposite, the greatest of all sins and refers to assigning partners or companions to Allah.

34. Arberry, p. 125.

35. Dawood, p. 149.

36. Arberry, p. 147.

37. Badru D. Kateregga and David W. Shenk, *Islam and Christianity: A Muslim and a Christian in Dialogue* (Grand Rapids: Eerdmans, 1980), p. 37, emphasis added.

38. Arberry, p. 75.

39. Ibid., p. 85.

40. Ibid., p. 48.

41. Ibid., p. 93.

42. Ibid., p. 220.

43. Ibid., p. 344; cf. pp. 102, 105.

44. Sura 23:104-05 in the George Sale translation (1734) as cited by Phillip H. Lochhaas, *How to Respond to Islam* (St. Louis: Concordia, 1981), p. 24.

45. Dawood, p. 241.

*46. Abdiyah Akbar Abdul-Haqq, *Sharing Your Faith with a Muslim* (Minneapolis: Bethany, 1980), p. 164.

47. William Miller, *A Christian's Response to Islam* (Nutley, NJ: Presbyterian and Reformed, 1977), pp. 82-83.

48. Arberry, p. 58.

49. Ibid., p. 143.

50. Dawood, p. 372.

*51. Josh McDowell and John Gilchrist, *The Islam Debate* (San Bernardino, CA: Here's Life Publishers, 1983), p. 172.

52. Elder, pp. 94-96.

53. Wilson, p. 20.

54. Elder, p. 59.

55. J.M. Rodwell, *The Koran* (New York: Dutton, 1977), p. 78.

56. Arberry, p. 274.

57. Abdul-Haqq, p. 159.

58. Wilson, p. 24.

59. Arberry, p. 111.

60. Dawood, p. 256, emphasis added.

61. Arberry, p. 93; cf. p. 98.

62. Dawood, pp. 212-22.

63. Ibid., pp. 367-68.

64. Arberry, pp. 198-99.

65. Ibid., pp. 139-40.

66. Rodwell, p. 471.

67. Arberry, p. 214.

68. Rodwell, p. 417.

69. Musa Qutub and M. Vazir Ali, "The Glorious Quran—The Unique Divine Document for Mankind," in *The Invitation*, Nov. 1987, vol. 4, no. 4, Des Plaines, IL: p. 1.

70. Arberry, p. 135.

71. Ibid., p. 229.

72. *Encyclopedia Britannica*, 1958 ed.

73. Morey, pp. 137-58.

74. Rodwell, p. 3.

75. Dawood, p. 253.

76. Rodwell, p. 499.

77. Arberry, p. 83.

78. Dawood, p. 254.

79. Shorrosh, pp. 201-19.

80. Ibid., p. 140.

81. Dawood, pp. 291-92; 101:194; Rodwell, pp. 473-74n; Arberry, pp. 63, 83, 138, 158, 185 (cf. 258), 187-88, 190, 314, 331, 348; see also Gleason L. Archer, *A Survey of Old Testament Introduction,* rev. ed. (Chicago: Moody Press, 1985), "Appendix on Errors in Koran," pp. 506-08.

82. Don Wismer, *The Islamic Jesus: An Annotated Bibliography of Sources in English and French* (New York: Garland Publishing, 1977); cf. Arberry, pp. 242-60; Dawood, pp. 324-32, 339, 348, 285, 175-81, 319, etc.; cf. Rodwell, p. 105.

83. Arberry, *Interpreted,* pp. 135, 229; see Q. 13.

84. Dawood, *Koran,* p. 365.

85. Ibid., p. 134.

86. Ibid., p. 294.

87. John Warwick Montgomery, "How Muslims Do Apologetics," in *Faith Founded on Fact: Essays and Evidential Apologetics* (New York: Nelson, 1978), p. 93.

88. E.g., Khalid Jan, in his attack on biblical authority in *A Human Bible* (draft), cites such biased sources as the Jesus Seminar's *The Five Gospels* and G.A. Wells, *Who Was Jesus?* while taking other sources out of context, cf. various Muslim Internet sites.

89. For an illustration, see John Weldon, "Letters to the Editor," in *The Athens [GA] Banner-Herald,* Oct. 2, 1989.

90. Available from the California Institute of Apologetics. Also see Morey's "Muslims and Their Logical Fallacies," *The Truth Seeker,* Jan. 1997, as well as other debates and materials, including those resources mentioned at the beginning of this section. The interested reader should also secure literature from American Islamic Societies, e.g., The Islamic Center, Washington, D.C., as it relates to their treatment of Christianity.

91. Arberry, p. 85, emphasis added.

92. Ibid., p. 35.

93. Dawood, p. 384.

94. Arberry, pp. 120-21.

95. Ibid., p. 122.

96. Abdul-Haqq, pp. 22-31, 38-46, 50-53, 67-73; Arberry, pp. 185, 199, 120-22.

97. Arberry, p. 130.

98. Stephen Neill, *Christian Faith and Other Faiths,* 2nd ed. (New York: Oxford University Press, 1970), p. 64.

99. Cf. Morey, pp. 129-32, 136, and our note no. 90.

100. Norman Geisler and William Nix, *A General Introduction to the Bible* (Chicago: Moody Press, 1971); cf. F.F. Bruce, *The New Testament Documents: Are They Reliable?* (Downer's Grove, IL: InterVarsity, 1981); John Warwick Montgomery, *History and Christianity* (San Bernardino, CA: Campus Crusade for Christ, 1982).

101. Geisler and Nix, p. 375; cf. pp. 238, 267, 365 66.

102. Morey, pp. 117-20.

103. Ibid., pp. 120-26.

104. Rodwell, p. 1; Alfred Guillaume, *Islam* (New York: Penguin Books, 1977), p. 57.

105. Miller, p. 52; Elder, p. 27.

106. Guillaume, p. 57.

107. Robert E. Hume, *The World's Living Religions,* rev. (New York: Charles Scribner's Sons, 1959), p. 229.

48

108. Guillaume, p. 56.
109. McDowell and Gilchrist, pp. 50-51.
110. Shorrosh, pp. 197-98.
111. Wilson, pp. 29-30.
112. Dawood, pp. 10-11.
113. Arberry, p. 41.
114. Ibid., p. 73.
115. Ibid., p. 46.
116. Ibid., p. 298.
117. Dawood, p. 304.
118. Chauncey Sanders, *An Introduction to Research in English Literary History* (New York: MacMillan, 1952), p. 160. Sanders is an associate professor of military history, Air University, Maxwell Air Force Base, Montgomery, AL. His comments were specifically in reference to the authenticity or authorship of a given text.
119. Reprinted in John Warwick Montgomery, *The Law Above the Law* (Minneapolis: Bethany, 1975), appendix, pp. 91-140.
120. Reprinted in *The Simon Greenleaf Law Review,* vol. 1 (Orange, CA: The Faculty of the Simon Greenleaf School of Law, 1981–82), pp. 15-74.
121. Irwin Linton, *A Lawyer Examines the Bible* (San Diego: Creation Life Publishers, 1977), p. 45.
122. John Warwick Montgomery, "Legal Reasoning and Christian Apologetics," in *The Law Above the Law* (Minneapolis: Bethany, 1975).
123. J.N.D. Anderson, *Christianity: The Witness of History* (Downer's Grove, IL: InterVarsity, 1970), pp. 13-14.